Why Monkeys Swing in th[e...]

A play by Claudia Lloyd
Based on the original picture book
Illustrated by Celestine Wamiru

Characters

Crocodile 	Lizard 	Tortoise 
Monkey 1 	Monkey 3 	Chameleon 
Narrator 1 	Frog 	Fish 
Monkey 2 	Hippo 	Parrot 
Narrator 2 	Elephant 	Warthog 
Tinga birds 	Lion 	

The Tinga birds and narrators are on-stage all the time.

Narrator 1: Once there was a time when monkeys didn't swing in the trees.

Tinga birds: The monkeys used to stay on the ground and play. They loved to jump and play all day!

Narrator 2: Those naughty monkeys **loved** to wind up Crocodile!

Crocodile, the three monkeys and Hippo enter.

Monkey 2: Let's pull Croc's tail!

Crocodile: *(crossly)* SNAP! Don't call me Croc!

Hippo: Careful, Monkeys! If you keep pulling that end, you will find that the other end has **teeth!**

Narrator 1: Hippo was right. Crocodile was one of the scariest animals in Tinga Tinga, and he didn't like being teased.

Crocodile: Grrr! Snap, snap, SNAP!

The monkeys exit. Lizard enters.

Lizard: What's up, Croc, my friend? You look snappier than normal.

Crocodile: Grrr ... I'm fed up to the teeth with those mischievous monkeys.

Lizard: You need a plan, Croc. Something to show those monkeys who's boss. Something you can really get your **teeth** into.

Crocodile: Hmm ... If you come up with a good plan, Lizard, I may reward you with an egg for your supper.

Lizard: OK, it's a deal!

Lizard and Crocodile exit. Eagle enters with big, flapping wings.

Narrator 2: Meanwhile, high up in the skies, Eagle had seen some big grey clouds. That meant The Big Rains were coming.

Lion and the three monkeys enter.

Lion: The clouds are nearly upon us. Every animal must find shelter.

Monkey 3: I knew Lion was going to say that. Lion **always** says that!

Lion: Monkeys, will you stop chattering? Remember the last time The Big Rains came? The river rose and you got stuck up the mango tree, didn't you? Well, don't let it happen again!

Monkeys: *(laughing)* We **knew** Lion was going to say that!

Tinga birds: Watch out! Look about! The Big Rains are coming!

Narrator 1: So all the animals went to find shelter from The Big Rains. All except the monkeys ...

Monkey 2: Everybody's gone! You know what that means?

Monkey 3: More mangoes for us!

Monkey 1: Let's get picking!

Lizard enters.

Narrator 2: But Lizard saw what the monkeys were up to ...

Lizard: Nice one! The monkeys are heading for the mango tree! Now I have a really good plan. That means eggs for supper! I'd better go and find Croc ...

All characters except the narrators and the Tinga birds exit. Crocodile enters and lies down. Then Lizard enters.

Narrator 1: Crocodile was dozing in the river.

Lizard: Hey, Croc! Lion says The Big Rains are coming. Remember the last time, when the monkeys got stuck up the mango tree?

Crocodile: I do, I do.

Lizard: And remember how the monkeys can't swim? If you told them you would save them, that would be a very good time to **catch** them!

Crocodile: Hmmm. Now that is a very good plan. What are we waiting for?

Lizard: **That** is what we're waiting for ... The Big Rains!

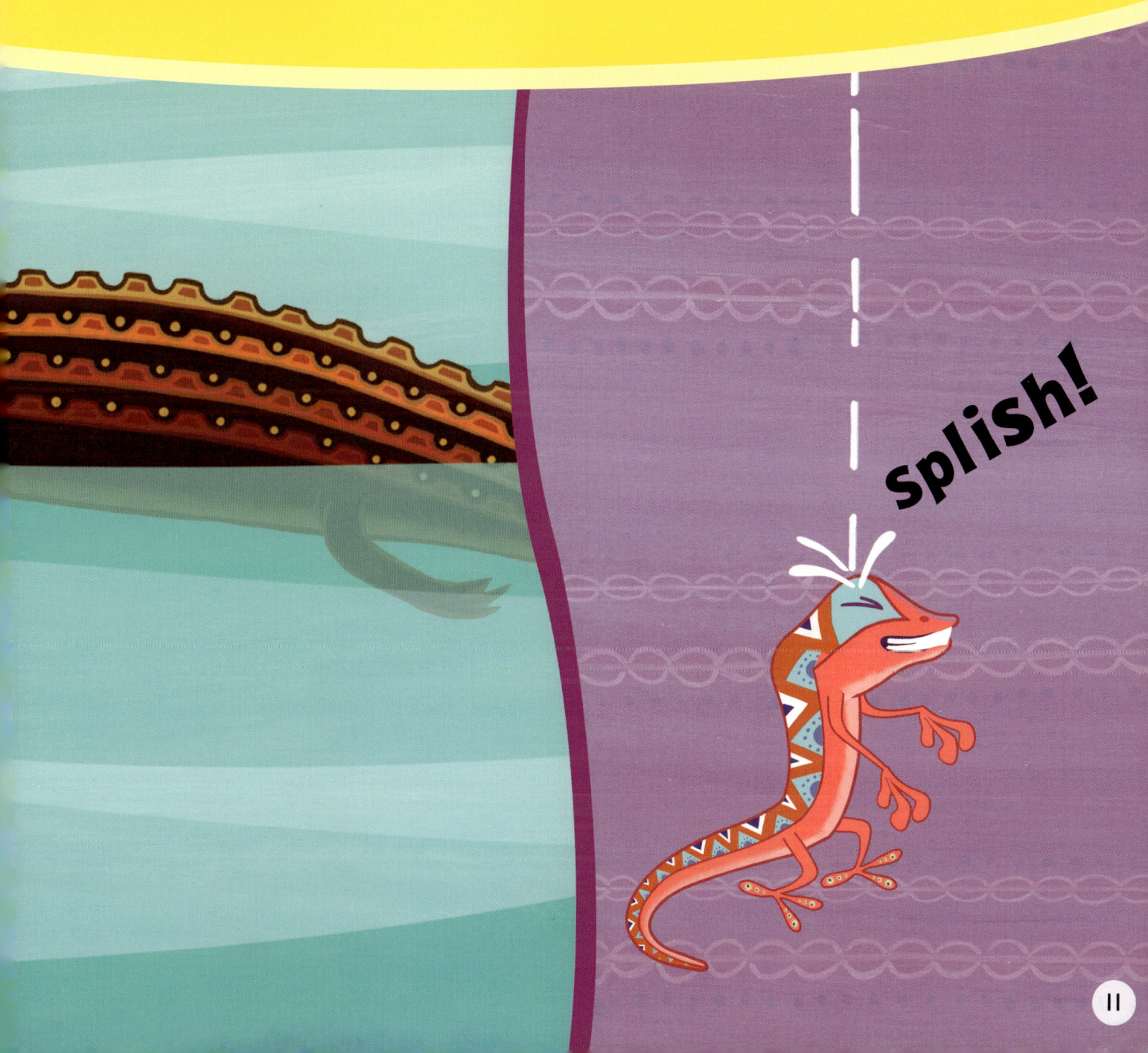

splish!

Fish, the monkeys and all the animals enter and sing The Rain Song.

Frog: Ah ha! Ribbit!
I love the rain.
It makes me cool.

Chameleon: I love the rain,
but I'm cool enough already!

Frog: We love the rain!
It makes things grow.

Hippo: I love the rain,
but I've grown enough already!

Tinga birds: Can't sing, can't sing!
It's too wet to sing!

Parrot: Let's sing and sing!

Tinga birds: You've sung enough already.

All animals: We love the rain …
We love the rain …
The rain …

Fish: I love the rain,
it makes things clean.

Monkey 2: I love the rain
when it turns the leaves all green.

Frog: I love the rain,
it fills my pond.

Hippo: Fills all the rivers
and the seas far beyond.

Tinga birds: Can't sing, can't sing,
it's too wet to sing!

Frog: Let's sing and sing!

Tinga birds: We've sung enough already!

All animals: We love the rain …
We love the rain …
We love the rain …
We love the rain …

All characters except the narrators, the Tinga birds and the monkeys exit.

Narrator 1: It rained and rained in Tinga Tinga. But even though the waters were rising, the monkeys kept picking mangoes.

Monkey 1: (*grabbing the biggest mango*) Look at that big, juicy mango!

Monkey 3: Let's save the best one for last.

Narrator 2: But the monkey dropped the juicy mango into the water.

Monkey 2: Oops!

Monkey 1: Uh-oh. Now we've been **really** silly.

Monkeys: Haraka! Haraka! Come quickly! Help! We're stuck up the mango tree!

Narrator 1: But then along came Crocodile and Lizard …

Crocodile and Lizard enter.

Crocodile: Jambo, Monkeys! Stranded up the mango tree again? What a terrible shame. Would you like some help?

Monkey 2: You'd **help** us, Crocodile? After all the times we've pulled your tail?

Narrator 2: Crocodile agreed to take the monkeys back to dry land, one by one …

Crocodile swims back to dry land first with Monkey 3 and then Monkey 2 on his back.

Narrator 1: … until it was the last monkey's turn.

Monkey 1: Haraka, haraka! Hurry, hurry! The water is nearly up to my feet!

Lizard: Not so fast, Monkey. Don't you think you should apologise to Crocodile for all the times you've pulled his tail?

Monkey 1: Dear Crocodile, I am very sorry and I will try never to tease you again ... never, ever, EVER.

Crocodile: *(moving closer to Monkey 1 threateningly)* Apologies are all well and good, but this time I want something more – **your heart!**

Monkey 1: My heart? Well, why didn't you say so? If it's my heart you want, you must both promise to look the other way. You don't want to see me take out my heart, do you?

Narrator 2: So while Crocodile and Lizard turned around, Monkey reached for the big, juicy mango.

Monkey 1: Ready! Here's my heart! But first, Crocodile, you must take me back to dry land. Then I will give you my heart.

Narrator 1: All the animals were really worried when Crocodile was bringing Monkey back to dry land.

The Tinga birds and Lizard enter.

Tinga birds:	Oh, poor Monkey! Oh, poor Monkey!
Elephant:	What **is** Monkey doing?
Tortoise:	Look! What's that he's got in his hand?

Warthog:	It's not … his **heart**, is it?
Tinga birds:	Oh, poor Monkey! Oh, poor Monkey!
Elephant:	How will he manage without his heart?
Tortoise:	I just hope Crocodile gets him back safely!

Narrator 2:	Monkey jumped off Crocodile's nose and gave him his heart.
Crocodile:	SNAP!
Monkey 1:	*(pretending to be at death's door)* Jambo, dear friends, always remember me …
Narrator 1:	But Crocodile was in for a surprise!
Crocodile:	Urrrgh! Yuck! This is not your heart! This is a **mango**!
Monkey 1:	Ha, ha! Sorry, Crocodile! I didn't have the **heart** to tell you! Better eat your mango and make it snappy!

Narrator 2: All the animals laughed and laughed.

Tinga birds: Funny old Monkey! Serves Croc right! Funny old Monkey! Serves Croc right!

Narrator 1: But Crocodile didn't find it funny at all. He chased the monkeys up into the trees!